THE AIR ABOVE MY HEAD

A Spiritual Journey

Cancer and me: 29 years and counting

by

Noa Ain

Copyright © Julia Ain-Krupa, 2020. All rights reserved.

No part of this book may be reproduced in any form or by any electronic or mechanical means, including information storage and retrieval systems, without permission in writing from the copyright holder.

First Edition
January, 2020

ISBN-10: 1-947373-11-0

ISBN-13: 978-1-947373-11-2

Photo credit for author picture: Gail Hadani

Printed in the United States of America

Typesetting: Bookman Antigua, 12 point

Publisher's note: The author's punctuation choices in poems and other passage have been respected.

Disclaimer: Some names, places, descriptions, and events in this book have been changed to protect individual privacy. Any similarity to actual persons or other circumstances is purely coincidental.

Lexingford Publishing LLC
www.lexingfordpublishingllc.com
Los Angeles   Miami   Hong Kong   New York

For those who forge their own path--

Foreword

More than 20 years ago, I faced my own struggle with cancer. In the midst of well-intentioned but fearful loved ones all around me urging me to do one thing or another, I chose a different path. Everyone thought I was making a terrible mistake. Just as poet Robert Frost advises us to choose *The Road Not Taken* in life, I did just that when it came to my health, and he is right in that it "made all the difference."

Now, as a doctor who works with patients with stage III and IV cancer who come to me from all over the world, I have the opportunity to invite them on a deeper healing journey down the path I chose to take. I get to introduce them to a broader perspective of the metaphysical aspects of their condition — that cancer isn't merely something in their life, but a response to it.

Noa's story, as chronicled in this book, of surviving and thriving for 29 years after receiving a cancer diagnosis, is an inspiration and invitation to everyone on a healing journey to choose their own path regardless of the road others have taken. It's a confirmation that when we have the courage to take the road less traveled, we empower ourselves with the knowledge that our decisions are being made based on what we intuitively feel is best for us and never out of fear. With this greater peace of mind and sense of control, we can focus more readily on the psycho-spiritual aspects of the healing process.

As a physician who has worked with hundreds of cancer patients, I am convinced that it was Noa's irrepressible spirit and courage to choose another path that allowed her to survive and thrive for so long after her original diagnosis. I tell all my patients with regard to longevity and healing that the disease isn't the issue, but how they relate to it. Noa saw her disease as something she had, not what she was. She chose to work with it rather than fight against it by constantly reinventing herself as challenges arose. Simply put, she chose to live…and she did, joyfully and abundantly. Clearly, that made all the difference for her, too.

Reading this book brought to mind one of my favorite poems, *Last Night/Is My Soul Asleep?* by Antonio Machado. To me, Noa is the embodiment of Machado's whimsical work. In it, he speaks of dreaming marvelous illusions of the heart being filled by the warmth of the sun, soothed by the waters of a crystalline stream, and as the seat of God in the human body. He describes how it's in the heart where our mistakes and failures are transformed into golden honey, and that the soul never sleeps, but watches and waits for us to call upon it for guidance.

Noa had the courage to dream marvelous illusions of health and healing, even when those around her were saying it wasn't possible. She intuitively knew that living a heart-centered life was the key to emotional and physical health. When we look at things from a loving perspective, it becomes clear that what appear to be mistakes and problems in our lives are actually working toward our greater good, and so we struggle less because our suffering has meaning. Most of all, Noa understood how to go within and access her soul for guidance instead of succumbing to fear.

It is an honor for me to write the foreword to this book because it will inspire readers in the same way I encourage my patients to be more proactive in their healing journey and open a path that will lead them to the guiding force within their soul. That's where the answers are. That's where they've always been.

Dr. Habib Sadeghi
Los Angeles
2019

PROLOGUE

When I was a student at Rasa Yoga, Ketul, our teacher, decided it was time to give a Halloween party where we came dressed as our problems. It was a great idea and a great evening. The celebration included lessons in belly dancing, delicious homemade food, music from many parts of the world, new students and old, everyone dancing their hearts out in their crazy outfits.

During the evening, my attention kept wandering to a very tall woman dancing with an equally tall man. As the party was winding down, I walked over to her.

"How can you dance wearing that huge heavy backpack? Why don't you put it down?" I said.

"I've been trying for years," she said.

PRELUDE

It was 1976, the year of the American Bicentennial, and Marcia Tucker (head curator of the Whitney Museum and later, founder of the New Museum) decided that to celebrate, she wanted to introduce the best of Young American Talent to the public. Her list included Phil Glass, Steve Reich, Laurie Anderson and me, singing and accompanying myself on the piano during a concert of my "Song Portraits." The others went on to become major forces in the music of this century.

And me?

I had fallen wildly in love with a Polish actor and a few days after my Whitney concert, left with him for Poland.

I stayed for six years, gave birth to our daughter, and worked at the Electronic Music Studio in Krakow. I became part of the wonderful Teatr Stu, with its magical director, Krzysztof Jasinski, where I wrote and directed a "Melodrama with Continuous Music" that was chosen as "Best Piece of the Year." It was a year in which the great theater director Tadeusz Kantor and Academy Award-winning filmmaker Andrzej Wajda were still working in Krakow. I was to be given Kantor's workspace for my own productions the following fall (Kantor had already left with his group for Italy), and I was busy making Krakow my home.

I felt I was an artist at last, free to be admired and sought after by some of the best composers curious to meet and talk.

At that moment, my Polish lover (now husband), decided it was time to try his talent in the larger world and with mixed feelings (I knew how hard it was to be an independent artist in America), the three of us said goodbye to his Polish family and left to live among my relatives in Manhattan.

Six years later (29 years ago), I was diagnosed with breast cancer and another journey began.

This is the history — of what happened, of the negotiations with my doctors, the creative work I never stopped making, of the spiritual growth and erotic refinement that for me seems to walk hand in hand with the cancer.

This is my testament to the fact that I have always believed that "tomorrow will be a better day." And it always has been (even when I had to skip a year or two from one day to the next), and I am still here.

This book is my gift to all who have asked me to tell them "how it has been possible to 'survive' so long?" Have I done anything different to "beat the odds" of this terrifying tragic disease—one must fight—one must fight until one's dying breath?

But, I say…

Not fight,
But understand…

Be compassionate
Love and accept it as part of you

The two of you
Together

Making not harmony,
But a cellular
Symphony…

Read these pages
Carefully
And

Listen.

WHAT HE FOUND

We were lying together, touching each other, full of the warmth, quiet and fullness that only loving sex brings. As he touched my left breast, he said, "What's this?"

"What's what?" I said, and followed his fingers with my eyes still closed.

A small hard lump greeted my touch.

"Maybe it will go away?" I said, a bit shocked to be brought back to consciousness. For the next few days, I would suddenly remember, hoping for smooth softness – but it was always waiting – small and round, filling my impatient heartbeat, disturbing my days and nights.

A few days later, I called my gynecologist – an older Polish doctor who was always there for those who couldn't pay full price. She felt the lump.

"I am sure it's nothing, but you're 45, old enough to begin getting mammograms. There is a clinic I know. Give them a call and make an appointment." She gave me their number, and a week later I had my first mammogram.

A nurse examined me and felt the hard place. Then, she made an appointment for me to return and see the surgeon on loan from one of the major New York hospitals. Several weeks later, I returned to enter the room of a slim, elderly doctor.

THE ICE KING

He introduced himself and told me to show him the "lump." He was a tall, white-haired man who projected infinite confidence, as if he had "seen it all." He palpated the lump, and began to laugh.

"That's a lump?" he said. "Forget it. We'll send you a notice to come again around the same time next year…"

He laughed again.

Much relieved, I called my husband, Olek, and happily, with our daughter, Julia, celebrated at the local Italian with pasta and cake, the next day returning to our life of hope and stress. (Olek was a wonderful actor, whose English was still limited… spending his days doing carpentry and paint jobs was very tough after success and adoration at his old theater in Krakow. But, our love was strong, and both of us braved on — he with his English and construction jobs, and me with my first opera.)

The following year, my "invite" arrived again in the mail. I went to the clinic and had my mammogram. This time I was seen again by the nurse and then by a doctor who was a recent Russian émigré. The nurse was concerned, the doctor worried, and then, once again, I was asked to return to be checked by the surgeon.

I returned a week later, and, once again, stood before the senior doctor. He felt the lump, laughed at me for still worrying and, slightly annoyed, said, "I told you, it's nothing. Next year, same time, you'll be back."

The year of my third mammogram was strained. My usual positive outlook on life seemed to have faded, and I felt a stranger in my own life. I kept falling asleep while working and felt, more and more, that I had nothing to give. That fall, my third invite came, but when I arrived at the clinic for my appointment, everything was surreal.

Immediately, I was ushered into a small waiting room where six women were sitting in different stages of despair, many crying, everyone exhausted.

The nurse ushered me into an exam room where the Ice King was waiting, now wearing a white doctor's coat. This time, the nurse stayed while I took off my blouse and bra. The doctor did not smile as he examined me.

"I still think it's nothing, but you're going to need to find a breast surgeon right away."

"That's it," he said and told the nurse to bring in the next woman.

"Wait," I said raising my voice. "Aren't you a breast surgeon?"

"Yes," he said. "But I am not yours."

"Why not?" I said. "You are the only one I know. Why are you so concerned this time and the other times you laughed? What's different? Why can't you be my surgeon?" By this time, I was so upset, I was almost yelling.

The doctor had stepped back. The nurse was coming towards me as if to restrain me when the doctor put out his arm to stop her and said "O.K. I will give you my card. Make an appointment, and I will see you at my office."

Fingers trembling, I slowly dressed and left.

Several days later, I saw him at the hospital where he worked. "I will first try to aspirate it to see if it's a cyst."

He put a big needle into my breast, but no fluid came out.

"You will have to have a biopsy just to be sure. I will make an appointment for you, and when I get the results, we will talk."

I left the hospital, shaking, and while traveling back to our apartment, a strength broke through my fear. I suddenly knew that this man could never be my surgeon. What would happen if I did have cancer? He didn't have a warm bone in his body or compassion in his heart.

A curtain came down.

At home, both of us weeping, my husband called his agent and found out that the universe was still with us. Having just completed his first film, he (and I) now had the best insurance that existed through Screen Actors Guild. In the days that followed, I had what became an intimate talk with the head of Second Opinion who said at last, "I am going to send you to the doctor that saved my mother's life."

DEAR DR. LEWIS

A highly intelligent older gentleman (on the president's list of best surgeons in the U.S.) sat behind his desk while his nurse took Julia into the next room to read. After hearing my story, Dr. Lewis told his secretary to call the clinic and ask them to immediately send over my mammograms. A week later, they still had not arrived. He told me to go downtown to the clinic and get them, "Do Not Leave Without Them." I went and, after hours of waiting, they gave me a large brown envelope. I was back the next morning, and after looking at the slides, he said he was going to schedule me for a biopsy at Roosevelt Hospital where he was the head breast surgeon. A few days after the biopsy, Olek, Julia and I returned to his office. As the nurse took Julia into the next room, Olek sat next to me.

I was all ears.

Listening.

Dr. Lewis said that it was cancer, and that it had progressed, as it should have been taken care of a long time ago. He said that since the lump was under the top of my nipple and all of the milk ducts spread out from that place, he would never know if he had gotten all of the cancer if he just did a lumpectomy, and so he recommended a modified radical mastectomy. My husband began to faint and the nurse ran for smelling salts. (Olek had just returned from burying his father who had died of lung cancer. This was way too much.)

I listened intently. I said, "I trust you to do what is best. When?"

"As soon as I can book an operating room," he said.

Olek was waiting in the car, trying to recover. I took Julia's hand and before we got in the car, I knelt down beside her.

"Mom," she said. "What's wrong? What did the doctor say?"

"Julia, I am sick. I have what Isabel's mother had. I don't want to die like she did, so the doctor is going to have to cut off my breast."

She was quiet for a moment, thinking her six-year-old thoughts. Then she said "Mom, if you have to, then do it and don't be afraid."

In shock, she didn't speak much for a few days. My darling, my Little Miss Freud. What a mistake I made. By wanting to be simple, to be clear, I broke her heart.

A few days later, Dr. Lewis cut off my breast. "No reconstruction" he said. "Leave it alone… You'll pay a better game of tennis."

"I don't play tennis," I said.

WOODSTOCK— ROBERTA'S HOUSE ON THE STREAM

Later that week, while Julia sat in the stream with our dear friends Len and Ramona, building dream houses out of rocks, I lay in the big bathtub, trees dancing, shadows on the walls, and, slowly, undid the wide white bandage that wound my chest, and wept and wept and could not yet look.

But already, I knew that was the end of the body I had known.
The end of baths together with my daughter.
The end of unconscious pleasure with my husband.

What I did not weep for, what I did not yet know, was that the huge scar was also a beginning, the beginning of a profound and extraordinary journey: Me and Cancer – finding out about each other, hand in hand, for the rest of this lifetime.

SHE WILL NOT LOOK

She will not look
At the ashes
Of the place
That suckled her gently
Home in this world that fed her
Wetly, quietly – every time her hungry voice cried out
Her voice cried out
Every time, every time

She will not look
At the ashes
That were her home
Softest pillow
Through which comfort came
The padded beat of my loving heart

O.K., I say –
Your place is hard now
The padding has been stripped away
Desperate, I'm still me
Still me.

"Yes, you are," she says. "And I love you so."

"But, if by accident I'd touch the place
That used to be my favorite
I'd feel my hand jump to my chest
Where my little breasts still wait to grow

Well, I say,
Let's look at it another way.

If the cancer that took our dear departed away had come sooner
We would not have had the time to stay
Breast to cheek
My life to your life pouring

So, if one day
In the midst of play
You should happen to run excited burst open the
Door to my private room
And see me naked
See the long diagonal flaming scar as if the
Doctor had X'd out half my chest

Don't turn
And run
And scream
And cry
As if my pain could make you die

Come close to me, and then you can
Hug me   and say

"Mom
I didn't know
It hurt you

So"

From NEXT SPRING, words and music © NOA AIN

DR. SCHWARTZ

The oncologist that Dr. Lewis sent me to was a Jewish Santa Claus.

A generous happy man,
A good photographer and a
Compassionate listener.

We met in his small office at the old St. Clare's Hospital.

"Dr. Schwartz, I don't believe that the chemical destruction of anything in the body can help the body become well again, so if you're going to give me chemo, it better be just a little bit, otherwise, I'll never come back."

As I said, he was a good listener. He heard me, and over the next six months, we met every few weeks for my infusions. I'd sip my fresh orange juice, and we'd talk about music and look at his photographs.

Afterwards, Olek and I would go out for a big meal, which somehow seemed to settle my stomach. I believe it was only towards the end of the fifth month that Dr. Schwartz began to give me the full dose. It was hard to take, but I made it through, Tamoxifen and all.

CHEN SHAN

The summer after my mastectomy, while Olek was busy rehearsing *Dracula* at Byrdcliffe Theatre, we continued our recovery at Roberta's wonderful home that jutted out over the Woodstock stream like a boat. I spent the days I didn't have to go into the city for chemo sitting in the garden while Julia built castles in the stream. While walking into town one afternoon, I suddenly saw a man dressed in saffron robes. We looked at each other and smiled. He introduced himself as Chen Shan, and told me he was a Chinese monk, and at that time he was living by himself on top of the mountain. He invited the three of us for tea in his simple room, and after he heard my story, he offered to help. He came to visit us several times at our New York City apartment, and we went together to Chinatown to buy the herbs he thought would help me feel better. Through all six months of infusions, I never lost my hair.

PHONE CALL

Unexpectedly, I received a phone call from my brother, Jonathan, a Harvard Medical School graduate who ran a large radiology lab in Denver. We had never been close, but even so, he was concerned and had asked Dr. Lewis to send him copies of my mammograms and other tests. He said, "You have a case, and all the evidence you need to win it. I've asked around and found you the best malpractice law firm in New York.

"Call them," he said, and I did.

VISION

Last night as I was falling asleep, I had a vision that before I was born, I was called up before an angel whose purpose it was to tell me what my life-path would be. The angel said, "In this coming lifetime, you will be born with a multiplicity of extraordinary talents, but you will be poor as a church mouse."

I began to weep. I cried and begged the angelic presence, "Isn't there anything that can be done? I will need money to live, to do my work, to pay my bills… Isn't there anything you can do to change my fate?"

The angel became thoughtful, and after a time of silence said,

"I will need to speak to a higher authority," and then, evaporated.

I waited impatiently, trembling in fear for what would soon become my worldly future for I was about to be born.

Then, the angelic presence re-appeared and spoke, "O.K. but it will cost you a breast."

"Deal," I said.

c/o Schulman & Roberts
Dear Mr. Roberts,

Thank you so much for winning my case. Now I will have enough money to live my life as an artist with the freedom to tell only the truth as I see it. No chains.

My very best,

Noa Ain

Prayer Rug #1

MASTER

You came
Made me tea.
Talked of the Higher Force
The Wider Way
Then,
Seeing I was shaking said,
"Come, I will drive you
To him."

You drove me up the mountain
Up Abbey Road
To Middle Way
To the small room
Where the man sat
Waiting.

This is him
Master of the Scream, you said.
I'll wait at the bottom of the hill, so I
Can't hear.
Hear what? I said, as you
Walked out the door.

The master was plain, dressed in a
Black sweater, jeans
He looked like anyone.

I saw him studying me
Watching the straight edge that used to be my
Breast
Watching my feet
The way I tried to hide my
Knees

Tell me, he said
All about it

I talked and talked
Till I was blue
Of the terrible two years
I'd been through
Let's not waste time
Do stand like this
Feet turned in
Head hung low
Just breathe and feel and speak to me
Look at me
I can't

Look at me.
I can't.

I let my head dip,
My toes curl in
Breathed deep, did as he'd
Said

Then from my way inside
From the bottomless place
A scream was born and rose
Layer upon layer
Fold upon fold
How he or she
Did this to me
AND THIS TO ME
AND THAT TO ME
And in that scream
An image came
A wall of red
"It's rage," he said
"It's pain," I screamed
"The place where they
cut off for good
A part of me"
"THE SAME" he shouted
Then he said,

"YOU'VE NEVER BEEN THE WOUND YOU THOUGHT"

I closed my eyes.
And with it came
Quiet things…
French castles at seventeen…
Luxurious gardens,
A man smoking a cigar, soft southern-voiced
Clavichord in the dusk…

Then came
Me holding you in the forest
Poor genius child with your wrists slashed
Helping you
Screaming for you
Trying to make your voices go away
So I could lead you gently back to town
Find a phone booth
Call for help

He left.
Practically disappeared out the
Back door.
I took my time
Gathered my things up
Wiped my face
Came slowly out into the
Summer sunshine.

A few seconds later,
My friend walked up the hill…
Everything smelled good
I could taste the honey the
Bees sucked out.

"Thanks," I said.

"Heard it," he said.

From NEXT SPRING, words and music © NOA AIN

Prayer Rug #2

NEXT SPRING

Next Spring,
I told my daughter
We'll all have an all-night party
Your dad and I will dance with you
We all will dance with you
All around the table
All around the table
Yes

After my
Left breast is re-born again
I'll get all those whose gifts of love carried us
Through those first hospital days

And dearest child,
You and I will plan the dance.

We'll take a
Walk
To buy a cake
That only the
Erotic baker sells
A two-breasted cake
Of beige and pink
Full of rum and juices and all things sweet

And when the
Guests arrive we'll cut the cake
With the grandest of gestures
From the nipple down
From the nipple down
The nipple down

And when only some crumbs
Are left to remind us
Of the extraordinary nature of this
Special occasion

We will all join hands
And we'll circle left
And my loves, we will
Dance and Dance,
Oh

From NEXT SPRING, words and music © *NOA AIN*

WHAT HAPPENED TO SEX?

The side effects of the chemo made it excruciatingly painful for me to have sex. Sex between us had always been fluid, exciting and fulfilling. But now, every internal movement was torture. I was desperate to return to the easy, relaxed passion of the past. My labia was so swollen I could hardly walk. No cream, no gel helped. I went from gynecologist to gynecologist, and finally ended up at the office of the head of gynecology at Roosevelt Hospital who said, "I don't even have to examine you. It's from chemo and Tamoxifen. I have women standing in line."

He laughed, "If you find anything that can help, let me know right away. Of course, the only thing that can help is estrogen, but for you it is so dangerous. On the other hand, there's a question of the quality of life." For me, these words meant that if I wanted to have wonderful sex again and keep my marriage I should consider taking estrogen even though it would probably kill me.

I left his office enraged, vowing that somehow, I would find a cure for my sex life that would not hurt me… and eventually, I did.

DR. DHONDEN

Dr. Dhonden, doctor of the Dalai Lama, gave me a recipe for herbs. I still remember my excitement when they'd arrive from Dharamshala, India, wrapped in plain brown paper and string with unknown stamps. I made the tea and drank it for the next year. It helped… some.

Some years later, an Ayurvedic douche brought to my attention by Ketul, my teacher of Rasa Yoga, brought the erotic back into my life full force. But by then, my marriage had fallen apart.

There had been too many changes— change of country, of language, death of both of our fathers. At this moment, Olek and I decided to live separately, and eventually divorced. Even so, we always remained friends and still consider ourselves family. Julia remained with me.

TAI CHI

I joined a friend in the study of Tai Chi with Sha Hang. The movements felt so natural, and often during class, as we moved in the fluid dance, I found myself trembling, not from tiredness or fear, but something new.

I did not understand then. Later, I grasped that this trembling was the beginning of what I did not yet know.

RASA YOGA

Through the years I was involved in Tai Chi, and later with Rasa Yoga, I began to be re-introduced to my body. I became a fairly regular member of the Rasa community, and slowly turned from someone for whom it was hard to bend, into a more flexible, softer woman. The mastectomy was followed by many difficult reconstructive surgeries (silicon implants, later TRAM-flap surgery in its infancy). It took years for me to begin to accept the physically new me.

Through these ancient practices and particularly, my gentle teachers of Rasa and the Bateman Method of yoga, I slowly began to be introduced to Ayurveda and a simpler more conscious way of eating.

Olek and I were still going through the pain and chaos of our divorce, and Julia was having her own hard times. I never knew what was going to happen next, and felt lucky to be able to work at home keeping my eye out for I never knew what, while writing my second opera. It was about Joan of Arc… her inner world and her outer journey, an opportunity to reflect on my daughter's painful struggle to find her way through the chaos.

Despite the desperation around and in me, my "spiritual self" began to wake up. Ketul's class had a very special atmosphere, and this helped to encourage my stirring. Rasa was a method that asked students to hum both as we moved into and held a pose. Humming amazed me. Being a musician, perhaps I was even more open and conscious than others, as the effect of the vibrations moving through me caused all but pleasure to fade. Over the four years I worked with this group, I had periods when a vibrational shiver would begin to move up my spine – it felt amazing, but no wishing or hoping would make it happen – it would come and it would disappear.

RETREAT

Those few summers I spent with my yoga community and Ketul at his New Hampshire Retreat gave purpose and health to the following months. The quiet, the simple health practices, the Ayurvedic cooking, the yoga while humming, was more beneficial than any doctor.

We began the day in the cold stream, chanting and moving arms upwards again and again like the rising sun, followed by a splendid silent breakfast, then yoga, then lunch in the fields. Late in the hot summer afternoons after a rest, we'd often take a path through the meadows to the tall pine guardians of the chill pristine waters below. One had to climb down slowly holding onto branches and, finally, gather courage and jump in. I did not have the strength to swim against the current, so I would stagger from rock to rock, listening to the others laughing and crying out with joy.

I both loved and was frightened by that wildness, the bees, the sharpness of the rocks, the depths, and the mystery. City-girl that I was—city-girl that I still am.

NEW SHOES

SCHOOL OF IMAGES
Exercise by Catherine Shainberg

Your shoes are worn out and you
Need to make a new pair. Make sure it's shoes that can go in the water.
What kind of shoes do you make?
Put them on, and step into the Stream.
Go to the mouth of the stream.
What do you see?

My feet soft-wrapped in green-leaf shoes, I step gingerly into the mountain stream. Surprised, I find it is easy to walk among the large rocks. I walk upstream against the current, pine trees to my left standing tall against the spreading sky.

Alone, embraced by the beauty of it all, I am pulled forward towards the unknown. Oh -- a faint low humming both familiar and unfamiliar joins the sound of birds and moving water.

Now, I quickly push ahead, and in the distance I see the movement of mustard-colored robes. Soon, I see monks standing in the deep water. Without looking, they part to make a path through which I walk.

As I approach the source of the stream, I see it is like an open mouth, above which a flat rock juts out. On the rock-shelf sits a wonderful icon. It shimmers in the light and I am full of its beauty. The words and sounds of the chanting are strange but I know their truth. I take my place at the rear.

Prayer Rug #3

A NEW CANVAS

It was 2001, one year after my *Joan of Arc* was performed at the Angel Orensanz Foundation on the Lower East Side of Manhattan. Rave reviews – visions left and right – many weeping – producing organizations said, "So beautiful, but what is it?" and my money was gone.

On the way to yoga, I went to visit Deborah, and sat there feeling hopeless.

"It's impossible," I said. "I've been devoted to music for so many years, but my heart is broken. I can't go on. What shall I do? Creativity is the only way I can be in this world." And Deb said, "Well, I like your paintings."

On and off over the years, I had painted, and took one course in my late 20s with Robert De Niro Sr. I still had some work hanging in my apartment.

"Why not paint?" she said.

It was time for Rasa. I left and walked around the corner, and as I got into the elevator, there was a notice on the wall, "Studio to share — call."

I went to class, afterwards wrote down the number, went to see it the next day and signed on.

I worked in that studio for several years, and in the beginning, I was often doing so while crying, because I was not composing. But after a month or two, I fell in love with painting, which has since become my open road.

Now, it is 17 years later, and my *Joan of Arc* will begin performances at Teatr Stu, in Krakow, Poland. It is scheduled to open November 2016, with 30 performances, and then, who knows? It's been a long wait.

THE AIR ABOVE MY HEAD

Lying in bed
I see the word *cancer*
In the air
Above my head

I had a commission for a new song cycle and was deeply involved, so when I saw the word *cancer* written in the air above my bed, I knew it was a message from my cells.

The next morning, I went straight to the office of my wonderful gynecologist, Dr. Elizabeth Hope. After examining me, she said, "You've been through a lot. Just to be safe, I think you should call your breast surgeon." Dr. Lewis had died years before, but through a close friend, I was given the name of Dr. Alison Estabrook. For the "occasion" of our first meeting, I put on a most beautiful pleated red dress so I was ready to greet "whatever happened." Dr. Estabrook was a small woman: self-contained—not warm, not cold—just listening. (Later she told me my dress had shocked her, and when our meetings had become warm and relaxed, she said, "I've never had anyone come to meet me for the first time dressed like that, especially if she had the intuition that breast cancer had appeared in her other breast.")

"You will need a lumpectomy, followed by chemo or radiation," she said. I sat quietly for a while, taking in the news. "Is it small or large?" I asked. "Small," she said. "In that case, I will have a lumpectomy and then go for Panchakarma at Living Ayurveda." I have no idea whether she had ever heard of Panchakarma, but I am sure she could tell that I was going to do what I thought was best. She did not try and change my mind or even discuss it. My decision had been made, and I knew by her acceptance that she could be my doctor.

I had the lumpectomy, and left for 10 days of extraordinary healing at Living Ayurveda with Susan and Jeff in Monterey, California. (I'd heard about them for years), returned 15 pounds thinner, having learned a lot about how to eat to rid myself of inflammation. When I returned, the mammograms were clear. I was followed at appropriate intervals for one year. The cancer was quiet. However, Ayurveda is a hard taskmaster in terms of diet, and after a while, I began to slip and eat things that were not on my dietary guidelines, and one year later, practically to the day, they found a new lump near the site of the lumpectomy. This time, Dr. Estabrook insisted in my following regular Western protocol and I had another lumpectomy followed by six weeks of radiation.

"Why don't you have another mastectomy?" she asked. "You have small breasts." "Well, I love the feeling of touch on my breast. I love sex and I want to feel attractive – no more missing body parts."

When the radiation was over, I decided that country living might help my body revive. I enlisted my dear friend, Judy Sacks, to drive upstate, and as we rounded a curve in a country road and the landscape of Amenia opened up before my eyes, I fell in love with a little old farmhouse. There was a "for-sale" sign out front, and three weeks later, I bought it.

So lovely. Embraced by the landscape: three acres, the remains of forest on the hill gave way to land that sloped down to a stream flowing out of wetlands beyond. In back, locust trees had been planted in concentric circles and in mid-summer, they'd burst into white blossoms of tiny orchids whose fragrance would drift through the green fields, and over the hand-wrought bridge that led to a wild meadow. There was yoga on the porch with the deer at sunrise. I'll never have that again.

The Wild Beast

LEARNING TO DRIVE AT 55

It didn't take long to find out that a little old farmhouse with a few acres is cheap only superficially. In truth, everything about the farmhouse was alive—wasps from the floorboards, snakes from the walls, everything moved. I had made a big mistake. There was no community. Isolation, snow, ice, friends mostly an hour's drive or more away, except for my dear friend Fred, and sometimes Ishi and his family. Three years later, I sold it and found what I thought was another dream come true. It was a double artist's loft with huge windows in the midst of woods right over the NY border in Connecticut. But something was very wrong. I didn't have the strength to open the garage door. I could only hold the phone or a paintbrush for 10 minutes a day. And every afternoon at exactly 4:00, I would feel that poison was being poured into my bloodstream and then, the pain in my lower right arm would begin. I couldn't sleep for six months.

For six months, I went from doctor to doctor—regular, alternative, but nobody seemed to find anything wrong. Finally, a physical therapist who came highly recommended, asked me who was my main doctor. When I told her, she said, "He's mine, also. I've known him for years. He's very good, but overworked and scattered. He'll never find out what's wrong."

And then she told me to go to Dr. Malik. "What kind of doctor is he?" I asked.

"He's a Naturopath," she said.

"What's a Naturopath?" I asked.

"It doesn't matter," she said. "He won't give up until he finds out what's wrong."

Dr. Malik, a wonderful young man, saw me at once. He turned off the phone, and asked me to tell him my story.

He listened intently for a long time and said, "I will give you a blood test, and then, following the signs, I will give you more blood tests until we know what is going on."

Two weeks later, I went back. "You didn't find anything, did you?"

"Unfortunately, I did. Your cancer has metastasized. You need to call your breast surgeon immediately and go back to the city at once."

One hour later, with $60 and one dress, I took the train to New York City, and by 11pm that night, had an MRI at Roosevelt Hospital. Cancer in my spine and bones.

The next morning, more tests, and by that evening, they began radiation to my spine. My doctors said, "It's the last minute." My surgeon said, "Try not to move. You could have a spinal cord injury," and the compassionate radiation oncologist, Dr. Ennis (who was an Orthodox Jew), came back to work to treat me even though it was the Sabbath. And everyone said "Call the Naturopath in Lakeville, Connecticut, and tell him he saved your life," which I did.

Olek and I drove to Dr. Malik's office, and he came down to meet us as I couldn't walk up, and we gave him armloads of flowers and all of us cried.

EIGHT YEARS AGO

Eight years ago, during the metastasis of my breast cancer to my spine and bones — during all that radiation, I decided that I needed only love, needed to be supported, to be rocked, needed comforting words and laughter, and slow, gentle yoga, soothing herbs, gentle hands and loving friends.

DEBORAH

Gentle, soft-voiced, deeply intuitive and compassionate, she taught the Bateman method of Yoga as if it were Tai Chi. The slower the better, never force, never push, every time anything hurts, back away, let it go – and slowly, approach again. By the end of her intimate semi-private classes of three or four students of all ages, I'd often fall asleep, I was so relaxed. We became private friends, and during radiation to my spine when my body would often go into spasms, she would come at night to where I was staying, massage me, and soothe my traumatized body and heart. Later, she became a coach and managed to guide both me and Julia through old angers and fears to a more constant, honest place — through the remaining fragments of childhood into an entirely adult and independent world.

DR. YAN

Dr. Yan (Jian Yi), my acupuncturist and friend for 20 years, always loving and available. Sure, his needles helped, and his "Magic Scar Cream." And throughout the almost eight years since the metastasis when my energy never returned, the herbal formula he invented "just for you," has allowed me to live a completely full life, full of music, friends, painting and love. Yes, Dr. Yan is another sturdy soul who, when I'd open my mouth so he could check my tongue always said with complete conviction, "Noa… you are un-beat-a-ble."

And I have always believed him.

WHEN THE RADIATION WAS FINISHED

When the radiation on my spine was finished, I was completely depleted and had to be taken in a wheelchair to a taxi. I was still staying with my friends, Judy and Michael, and for the first few days, all I could do was sleep. Two days later, Julia came for breakfast, took one look at me and said "Mom, your left eye looks funny."

Judy, a nurse as well as an artist, said, "Mmm… maybe it's a sty?"

By the next morning, we all knew it was something "special," as by then, I felt intense pressure in my head.

The eye had begun to look as if it was going to pop out of the socket. Dr. Goel (my oncologist) said, "Go immediately to the emergency room at Roosevelt."

We did, waited many hours, and by late that night, they did an MRI on my head, and made preparations to begin radiation on my eye. By the next day, the cancer had moved to include the other eye. My face was so swollen, I felt like Cyclops.

"It's the last minute, the last minute," all the doctors said. I had radiation daily on my dear eyes—ah—so, so much light, they had made me a mask with cut-outs for my eyes and mouth and the mask was snapped down to a table so I couldn't move. Nowhere to run, nowhere to hide. I hummed my way through each radiation, kept telling myself, it was only a few minutes a day, anyone could take that.

"Can you stop it?" I said to my determined and excellent Indian oncologist, Dr. Goel.

"We're trying," she said, and somehow, together, we did.

I was on high doses of steroids for my eyes, and I began to suffer a steroid psychosis. I gave everything away except my paintings, music, and a few things my mom had given me (by that time she was 98, and had forgotten how to use the phone. I saw her so little in the last two years of her life because I was too sick to take the train. Mostly, I went there when Olek drove. Beloved mom—the last time I saw her, I lay on her bed while she sat beside me in her wheelchair and rubbed my knee—looked up at me through her glasses, smiled and said,

"You know, you're my bestest?" I weep and remember— mom—always "true blue.")

Yes, I had given everything else away, put myself in the arms of the universe, and spent the little money I still had – all of it. By this time, I was staying at Tana's apartment, slept in her bed, drove her and her roommate, Anne, as well as Julia and anyone else who cared, crazy. I was a lunatic. Luckily, Tana found me an available apartment downstairs, and I moved out just in time to save our friendship.

Slowly, I began to feel better and, as I did, I began to realize I had no money left.

Julia was amazing: A full-time job, shopping for food, cooking for me, bringing friends and cousins to remind me that my life still mattered.

Then, a miracle:

Dear friends offered to support me for one year until I got back on my feet again (fingers crossed), and slowly, I began to gain strength.

MY GARDEN

I had always imagined that at one time of my life I would have a wonderful garden

I realized I already had it
That my friends were my
Flowers and my garden

And this most exquisite realization,

That I
Who had never liked to need to be needed
Could not go on without love
That others need for me as well as our love for each other nurtured me
Like rain
Like sun

And then
I understood the truth was
Just that I'd
Always been afraid
And that
At last,

Had changed.

TRUDY

As my body slowly began to wake up, I came back to my desire to create.

Then again, Trudy came through.

Wonderful friend, soprano, actress.

"Noa, I think it's time you write another song-cycle for me. Here are some ideas – pick one and begin – here's a check for half."

I picked Dante… Vita Nova.

But the fluid that filled my head after the radiation made me partly deaf. I had to turn my head and put an ear to the piano to hear anything. And, in the end, I had to exchange pianos three times in order to find one loud enough for me to hear the sounds.

It was slow, composing again.

Trudy arranged for me to have lessons in Italian with a master of the ancient text in order to write up-to-date English lyrics that honored the original.

It worked, and when Trudy finally performed the songs, the bravas filled the church.

NOW

It is the 29th year— me and cancer. I had taken all drugs available except the ones they "save" and advertise as often extending life for "at least a month," the ones they call "last chance," the ones for which they charge $5,000 a month (unless you have the right insurance, and your oncologist knows how to apply for a special price, then you might be able to get it for $4,700 a month.)

Does this mean that only the rich can live?

I wasn't interested, didn't want a pill that changed the color of my skin, and made rashes happen, and wasn't interested in chemo dripping into my veins for hours at a time, and then, somebody sweet rubbing my feet, or getting Graham Crackers or an old ham sandwich, guaranteed to make you feel worse.

The conundrum was and is:

I am feeling great and have fine energy. I have three important deadlines I will meet in the next three weeks, and have plans for placing my music and paintings in the world, that I don't intend to give up.

I was and am confused.

What or whom do I trust?

The cancer markers or my body?

I was still on an Ayurvedic diet, and for the last two years, had added straight-ahead, relaxed Dr. Bloom, a doctor of Functional Medicine. When I asked him why I kept getting breast cancer, he said, "It is because your estrogen (my cancer is estrogen-receptor positive) cannot leave your body. In order to leave the body, estrogen needs to be made liquid and that happens in the liver. Since your liver is not functioning properly, the estrogen builds and builds and then your cancer returns."

He told me to stick as much as possible to the Ayurvedic diet, adding a drink that keeps my liver in good shape, plus a few supplements.

It helps a lot.

So, since I have been working with him, I have mostly "toed the line."

But now, I was afraid, afraid to not do Western medicine, and afraid to do it.

Then I had a dream.

DREAM OF DOWN

I am standing at the top of a high outdoor cement staircase, and I know I must descend.

To my left, families of Orthodox Jews are ascending. Each family holds hands-- the husbands with the wives, the wives with the children, the children with each other. All are dressed for the Sabbath, and even though there are many children, they climb in silence.

As I descend, they divide to give me room to pass – no touching.

As I come towards the last step, I can see the ground is wet and muddy, and the building in front of me reminds me of the communist block houses I saw while living in Krakow. I step off the staircase into the muck so briefly that I almost don't mind.

As if transported to another realm, I find myself standing in the lobby of a white cement entrance room full of garish lighting, but I don't mind because for now, I find myself standing on solid ground.

Oh. To my left I see Melody's secret husband, Eli, a fearful, handsome, shy young black man with a scar across his right cheek. He smiles his sweet smile and speaks to me without words, and I can almost hear his sound pass between us. There is a shift, and amazed, I see that his true face is the face of Buddha.

Now, he speaks with great deference to someone on my right.

I look where he is looking, and see a man who, from his waist down is seated on the ground—his bottom half is missing. I am aware that Eli speaks to the half-man with so much love and respect – I look again, and now I can see that this man's face is also the face of Buddha.

The mud, the plainness, the ugliness of the entranceway in which we stand fades away.

A FULL LIFE

PORTRAIT…DEATH OF FRED

"Oh, Fred" she said. "I hate to weed.
My dad always wants me to help in his garden, but
I never want to and then he gets angry and thinks I'm lazy."
And Fred said, "How can you hate to weed?
It's all about having what you need so you can
Be free to
Love it."

"What? You love to weed?" she said.
And Fred said,
"Tell me, Julia…do you have your little radio? Your
Coffee and your folding chair? And what about the small wooden
Stool to set the things you need on? Oh, and some chocolate and a
Cigarette or two?"
We listened and we laughed like crazy because he always knew
Exactly what was
Needed to make anything work.
Knew enough to take distance take in the bigger picture bring it all
Into focus so you could enjoy the
Wonder without worry.

For him, after weeding, there was always a choice between
Hammocks to take a snooze in when work in his
Great garden masterpiece was done. And for an hour or two, he would
Lie there surrounded by the flowering glow he'd planted in
The hot afternoon or sometimes
In the evening he'd lie there to
Take in the
Moonglow and daydream of India and subtle saris coloring the
Fields and love
Still to be fulfilled.

Coffee Chocolate and Cigarettes
All day long, Real Food
Only in the evenings-
He never waited, but
Lived it out,

Sucked in pleasure, inhaled through and through-
Held it loosely in the palm of his hands
By-passed tears, turned it all into laughter

No-one else, ever
Like you

Beautiful man-
Somewhere between this and that
Always found the right angle to
Look at life through

Like when I was first arranging my loft upstate
When I lived upstate near you, you said,
"Hang your big red diamond painting on the furthest wall"
We looked and decided there was
Still more to do.
Even when the bed was covered in silk
And the large kilim laid on the floor,
You grabbed the corner
And pulled it a little to the right
Just enough
Because you knew
That that would bring the space
To life,
My Room
Now full
Of two

Your vision
My color
Our dialogue

Dearest Fred,
Miss you forever.
No-one like you,
Never.

Fred died a few weeks ago, napping on the sofa,
Looking out at the garden he'd made. It was not
Yet spring, and he was dreaming.

MARRYING MY SELF

During the six years I lived in Krakow, I wrote and then directed a melodrama with continuous music. The main character (a woman in her late 30s) wore an old wedding dress, as she had struggled for years to make sense of her birth family who populated both her waking and dream life, who not only participated, but seemed to direct her every move. She antagonized them, adored them, understood and did not understand them. Their words and voices haunted her inner and outer worlds.

Some emotional progress is made in the course of the performance of *Leaving Home* (*Czas Na Uwiegi*). In the last scene, her mother, father, her younger self and brother form an audience who watch while she (true bride at last) slowly takes off her veil to a recorded web made of audio fragments of the family's favorite sayings. However, even though their words and thoughts are still repeating in her head, all of them are now sung/spoken only in

Her Voice
At Last.

It has been a long engagement.

Years before I met Olek, I had a recurring fantasy of marrying myself in New York City's Central Park.

A dream of public commitment
No divorce in sight
But,
I never had the ceremony.

This long engagement…
Getting to know me.

As I see it now, there were 6 big steps…

1 Studying piano with Seymour Bernstein
2 Studying composition with Hall Overton
3 Studying painting with Robert De Niro Sr.

4 My marriage to Olek and all that followed
5 Giving birth to Julia and all that followed
6 Cancer, which has turned out to be my major life partner. And, as in any love-match, our relationship keeps shifting.

I've been working at it quite consistently lately,
And it seems, it's getting more stable.

Living beyond all reasonable expectations
29 years

Cancer now in my spine and bones, after-effects of radiation on my eyes

Learning to stand on my own two feet.

FOREVER, TANGO

My approach has shifted. I have always divided my attention and my medicines.

Both Western and Eastern have supported each other, and I was lucky to find doctors who were willing to collaborate, to listen, to help, but not to manipulate my choices.

And through it all, my body has known better, has helped me find the perfect way forward for me.

But now, it was late. Now, the power of freedom of choice, of medicines, of the road ahead seemed completely up to me. I kept on with the program set for me by Dr. Bloom, Beth, Jeff and Susan, my Ayurvedic practitioners, and the last hormonal suppressant that Dr. Goel felt was still somewhat helpful.

But my cancer markers continue slowly to rise…

Through the suggestion of an old friend, Eleanore Ament, I added low-dose Naltrexone. I felt very well, but my cancer markers kept creeping up. Dr. Goel kept repeating that I must add chemo.

I was so conflicted, because the only ones that were still available for my 4th stage late condition had terrible side effects, and here I was – still feeling and looking great.

Yet, Dr. Goel warned me not to wait too long.

A wonderful new friend, Amy Andersson, who had lived in Germany for years and was familiar with their treatments for cancer, told me that there was a new kind of chemo called Metronomic Chemo.

I told Dr. Goel that this Metronomic Chemo was the only chemo I would consider. It seemed to me to make so much sense, a pill every day for the rest of your life. No fantasy of killing the cancer, but keeping it "under wraps," incapable of becoming more brutal, and allowing the patient to live their life fully with few or no side-effects. As I read about it, it seemed to me to be a homeopathic dose.

Dr. Goel was open to it, and said she would look into it, which she did.

I have begun this new kind of chemo… this treatment that had been developed for the poor. But in the U.S., even this was financially forbidding. First, I was told that my everyday pill would cost $500 per month. I said, no way.

Again, Dr. Goel came through and called an organization that now gets it for me for $50 per month - a lot better, but part of me still objects to the price.

I have just begun this metronomic chemo, and my body is still surprised.

I still don't feel like myself — somewhat disconnected, as if I don't care —

Which I do.

DEAREST JULIA

Dearest Julia, holding my heart in her heart

Always Olek, Rysiek, Gienek, Elzbieta, Boleslaw, Baba dead or alive,

Always my mom whether here or there Sam and Jonathan, always Leah, Judy Michael Tim and Tracy, Deborah and family, Claudia Jessup and Jon Richards and family, Gail and family alive or already gone, Amy and family still here or already there, Sara Deborah Jacobsen Miriam Bobby, Rachel and Hilton, Hilary and all her beloveds, Beth Murti and Foster, Theo Susan and family dead or alive, Tana and all her beloveds here or already there, Nili Esther Natty and family and dearest Raphael no matter where, Fred dead or still here, Andrew and Julia now and then, Scott Pamela and Leib, Judy William and Sam, Mariko and children, Ishi and family, Randy and family, Rande Bernice Joel and family, Catherine Sam and the other already gone, Burt and all the generations of dearest aunt Ann, Vincent and Zahra, Peter Sue and family alive or already gone, Eva Johansson and the generations, Hadassah, Sophie and family, Art Bryant always remember, John Cazale friend forever, Krzysztof and family, Teatr Stu always remember, Franzi and family may her dreams come true, Elzbieta Czyzewska, Bolek Greczynski and his mom Stasia dead or alive, Janos Randy and family, Florika long ago, Dr. Bloom and family, Susan and Jeff, Barbara Rose, Seymour Bernstein, Hall Overton and the dream of music, Olga Szwajgier and daughters, Christian and Sheila, Olga and Janusz Stoklosa and family, Verushka Joanna and family, Naomi and Peter near or far, Didi and family, and all those who have passed through but have left their mark, Bonnie and her far away love, always Franek, Anya Michal and family and more to come.

The Dancer

BETH

Ayurvedic practitioner, Body-Mind-Centering, meditation instructor, Yoga teacher, hands-on work, and much, much more.

"I have an aversion to the term "healer" — so pretentious — as it is always the universe, the divine Shakti, that does the work. We're all just along for the ride."

KUNDALINI RISING

THE UNKNOWN TREMBLING

Like everything of value in my life, finding the source of the "unknown trembling" (which first happened in Tai Chi through the movements, next in Rasa Yoga through humming) has been another extraordinary journey.

PRIVATE SESSIONS WITH BETH

When I began to see Beth privately, I was involved with a man I could not live with and I could not live without. For the first time, I was erotically obsessed and the thought that it should end would bring suicidal thoughts. During my meetings with Beth, we often spoke of a deeper reality to sexual connection and obsession. That it is never just being with a particular partner that brings us to ecstatic heights, but it is what our body is capable of. When I understood this, I finally was able to let him go.

Then, my relationship to my self began to transform again. I would be driving somewhere, or painting, or sitting on the subway, and seemingly "out of the blue," I would have a series of spontaneous orgasms. I managed to "keep them under wraps," and could always stop them, but making them happen was not under my control.

I again went to Living Ayurveda, to Susan and Jeff, for Panchakarma. Now, it was after the metastasis and again, it was enormously helpful, learning to eat even more thoughtfully so that no new inflammation occurred, becoming more conscious. Letting go of fears allowed me to become ground fertile enough for the next step.

CANCER AS A DIALOGUE WITH KUNDALINI

I continued working privately with Beth and practiced moving through my body as a map of inner vision, learning to understand and translate the images that came up during our work, learning to create inner space to let my body spontaneously give birth to the essential life-force that lies within that emanates through the main channel and slowly reveals itself in the beginning by rising up.

And then, I began to notice something amazing…that when the cancer "rises up" it is always preceded by a rise in desire.

In the beginning, I always experience it as sexual and long for a partner. But more and more, I am quickly aware of it and can "catch it," and begin to "work with it."

I sit, eyes closed, and focus on a sound vibrating mid-forehead. Then, I let the vibrations move like water to encompass more and more of my body. The cells react quickly, and the feeling-image is as that they are included in the sound-vibration, they "stand at attention," until my entire body is vibrating as a cellular orchestra sounding

At
The
Unison.

Then, all of me, all thoughts, all hardness, all boundaries disappear, and I am, I exist only in a transformational state where nothing negative, no pain, no past, and no future, exist.

SACRED MEDICINE

If you're ripe, a guru can open your third eye by touching the exact place mid-eyebrows with the tip of a peacock feather. It's not the place or the peacock feather, but the intention that, if recognized at last, awakens who you really are. Not magic, but lifetimes of Sacred Practice is transferred from the guru to you in that moment, that is, the transference occurs if . . .

If you are conscious and your own practice (whatever it has been), has brought you to this place of fertile ground
Then, you will receive the teaching of the teacher
No matter what religion you have belonged to
No matter what traditions have formed you until this moment,

Beth is this.
As if she had a cold and staying close, you catch it, but it does not go away. The student who is ready does not catch illness but Sacred Treasure
Kundalini rising up to meet the challenges you face.

Born in a housing project in Brooklyn.
Granddaughter of Rabbis, with no Jewish education in this lifetime, her apartment is full of thangkas, floor piled with worn Afghani rugs, framed fragments of exquisite fabrics, photos of the inside turned out, marvelous manifestations of lost architecture,

Follower of the Medicine Buddha, she works accompanied by silence.
Distant chanting, she places her fingers at the exact points necessary to open the central channel in order to let the main life-force flow freely.

This after tea, dried fruit and laughter, this internal shift begins and in a breath beyond knowing, you are gone.
The inner flower has opened
Kundalini has risen and you are fully now

Her gift, this flowering.

ICON OF THE RED MADONNA

THE GATHERING

Beth took a large crystal singing bowl and placed it gently on my belly as I lay on the rugs surrounded by bones and deities. I closed my eyes to let the vibrations of the sound penetrate as she slowly rubbed the stick over the outer surface of the bowl.

"I don't need it, Beth – I can hear the sound without the bowl. I can feel the vibration just from the sound I hear. And anyway, it is too heavy."

She gently lifted it off, and I focused, I focused on the sound resonating high up in the middle of my forehead, the place of the inner eye.

Suddenly, I remembered what I'd heard and read about cancer, that it begins when some cells leave the fold, go their own way in errant patterns, thus infecting the surrounding cells, pulling them away from their original purpose into a darkening otherworld.

"Beth…what would happen if I slowly bring all the cells into the same sound vibration, so they would all be singing in synch, like a cell orchestra, would the cancer go?"

"Why not?" she said.

She moved back, and I focused on letting the sound vibrate through all of me, bringing attention to each new place without letting go of the old, working my way downward, keeping my third-eye-place as the center of attention.

Joy filled me. Fear left me. Over the next weeks as I continued my practice of "gathering in," I began to feel what I can only describe as the wind of the world expanding my breath, pushing my ribs outward.

Later, my stomach would emanate a light – dull, at first, but slowly brightening – filling my body in orgasmic ecstasy and with each sensation, announcing its presence, and the experience has continued to morph as time passes, every time more eloquent, more exquisite.

Would it cure the cancer?

I didn't even think about it, but I can tell you this –

The moment I began this practice of "gathering in," fear left me and a calm joy took its place.

That is, whenever it came to me, unexpectedly, as Beth had cautioned me not to try and "do it," but to let it "do me." Sometimes it came when I was on the subway or walking down the street, or…

And maybe, just maybe, as I move more deeply into the sound vibrations, the cancerous cells will be pulled back to sing with the rest.

In the cell body that is me, that is mine in this lifetime.

THE VISITOR

EPILOGUE

I am not special. The possibility for healing exists in all of us. The way opens when the student is not overly hopeful, but finds a balance between

Passive – you Find the way

    And

Active – you Make the way

Consider your Burden as you would a Mystery, and Consciously follow the Clues as they Reveal Themselves, One at a time. At many points in your journey (often when you've almost given up hope), the Right Teacher will appear and help point the way forward.

In time, your burden at last will open and
Inside it will be the Key to your Healing.

LIKE THIS.

THE HOLY TRIO

MIND, BODY, SPIRIT

TRANSFORMED IN THE

FLAME OF

INNER TRUTH.

Afterword

On the morning of January 11th, 2019, after a brief but intense period of acute illness, my mother, Noa Ain, took her last breath. Following a long journey depicted in this book, and after many years of enthusiasm for life and terrific joy despite her struggle, Noa succumbed to her cancer, moving on to her next journey. She left this world surrounded by love, and cared for by an extraordinary medical staff. She was not afraid or in pain, only frustrated that she could not have more time, as she still had so many projects underway, and felt that her life's work was not yet complete. And yet through her music, her art, her writing, and through us, her spirit persists.

For many years, I asked my mother to write a book about her experience with cancer. *People will be interested, will learn*, I told her. She dismissed my request, forever concerned with living and with being in the present. But eventually, she took the time to write *The Air Above My Head,* and I am so grateful that she did. Time has shown that her experience can benefit others, and I believe that this book inspires a new perspective, just as my mom's presence did for those who were lucky enough to encounter her on this earth. It is also an opportunity to hear her voice.

Noa left this world knowing that her book would be published, and that people would be touched by her experience, and by the beauty of her work. She was an extraordinary person, and I say that both as her daughter and as her student of life, as well as her friend. I wish she had more time. We had so much left to share. We continue our adventure from a new vantage point, and as she always said, "our love exists beyond time." This world is a dimmer place without Noa's presence, but through this book, through her artwork and through her lasting love of life, she lives on.

Julia Ain-Krupa
New York City
January, 2020

Additional Acknowledgements

Sincere thanks go to Gail Hadani, Rebecca Curtis, and Arthur Bell at Lexingford Publishing for helping to make the publication of this book possible. Thank you to Claudia Jessup and Jon Richards for their editing skills. Profound gratitude to Dotan Malach, for his love and support, and to the dear friends, family, doctors, nurses, and all of the strangers whose random acts of kindness and generosity helped to make this experience possible.

New York Times Obituary

Noa Ain—Composer, librettist, painter and lover of life, Noa Ain (nee Susan Ain) took her last breath on Friday morning. With her warm, vibrant, larger-than-life personality, striking style, and ever- painted red lips, Noa touched everyone she met. A graduate of The Juilliard School, she studied composition with Hall Overton, Seymour Bernstein, and Nadia Boulanger, analysis with Stefan Wolpe, and painting with Robert De Niro Sr. Her extraordinary talents were honored with an Obie Award (Metamorphosis in Miniature, directed by Martha Clarke), the Stephen Sondheim Award, and 14 ASCAPS, including Best New Composer on Broadway for her music for Mourning Pictures, by Honor Moore. Her music theater pieces were presented at Teatr Stu in Krakow, Poland, the Brooklyn Academy of Music, Carnegie Hall, the Houston Grand Opera, St. Ann's Warehouse, the Whitney Museum of American Art, and on countless other stages; her stunning visual works grace the walls of homes around the world; yet her greatest talent was her gift for life. Noa inspired those around her with her joie de vivre and devotion to art, despite struggling with cancer for over twenty-nine years. She lived well and did not consider herself a survivor, but rather a resilient person who chose to not live in fear, remaining instead forever engaged with her artistic projects and dreams, and friends, and strangers, and her daughter, Julia.

She wrote a book about her experience with cancer as a spiritual journey, *The Air Above My Head: Cancer and me, twenty-nine years and counting* (forthcoming from a California-based press), which depicts the unique ways in which she managed to work with her illness, collaborating with both healers and practitioners, as well as Western doctors, co-existing with her illness in an unusual and successful way. Those who knew her are heartbroken to discover that, once and for all, her spirit could no longer triumph. During a recent hospitalization, a young resident showed interest in Noa's book. With her usual openheartedness, Noa sent him the manuscript as soon as she returned home--she always knew that time was precious, and never wasted, or waited, a second. Upon reading the manuscript, the resident wrote Noa an email remarking how impressed he was by her unique approach to illness. "You are someone I will tell my children about," he said, and Noa gleamed at this kind remark. For those who knew her, either intimately or in passing, there is the heart-wrenching declaration, "I just cannot imagine a world without Noa!" She loved people, and she lives on in those who loved her, and in her beautiful work. She leaves behind her beloved daughter, Julia, her son-in-law, Dotan Malach, her ex-husband and forever friend, Olek Krupa, and a close, yet ever-widening circle of loved ones.

Published in *The New York Times*
Jan. 16, 2019

Remains of the Temple